Elias Hill
101 Dad Jokes: Christmas Edition
Copyright 2017
Self-published, Tiny Camel Books

Tiny Camel Books
tinycamelbooks.com
tinycamelbooks@gmail.com

101
Dad Jokes
Christmas Edition

December, 2021

Robb,
Happy St. Nick's Day!
Keep laughing,
Kram & Nerak

By: Elias Hill ☺

Illustrations By: Katherine Hogan

What language does Santa Claus speak?

North Polish.

Why don't we ever hear about Olive, the 10th reindeer?

There's no Olive the reindeer.

You know. Olive, the other reindeer, used to laugh and call him names...

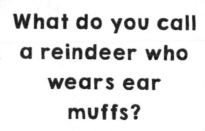

There's nothing like the joy on a kid's face when he first sees the video game box

containing the underwear I got him for Christmas.

Why is Christmas just like a day at the office?

You do all the work and the fat guy with the suit gets all the credit.

Two snowmen are in a yard and one turns to the other and says,

"I don't know about you but I smell carrots!"

What do you call a broke Santa?

Saint Nickel-less.

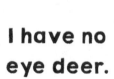

The Gingerbread Man saw a doctor for his sore knee.

The doctor said, "Have you tried icing it?"

Knock knock.

Who's there?

Gladis.

Gladis who?

Gladis not me who got socks this Christmas!

I told you all I wanted for Christmas was a gas grill.

I know but you'll look so nice in this sweater. What did you get me?

A gas grill.

What does Santa bring the naughty children?

A set of batteries with a note that says, "Toys not included."

Where does Santa go in the summer?

The North Pool.

How do sheep greet each other at Christmas?

"A merry Christmas to ewe."

Who tells the best Christmas jokes?

Reindeer. They sleigh everytime.

What do you get when you cross a snowman and a vampire?

Frostbite.

What's the difference between a reindeer and a knight?

One slays the dragon, and the other's draggin' the sleigh.

How does a sheep say "Merry Christmas"?

"Fleece Navidad!"

What happened to the man who stole an Advent Calendar?

He got 25 days!

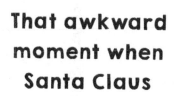

That awkward moment when Santa Claus

has the same wrapping paper you do.

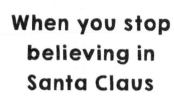

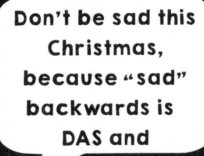

What's red, white and blue at Christmas time?

A sad candy cane.

And so the three wise men visited the baby Jesus and gave him gold, frankincense...

Can we open presents now?

But wait, there's myrrh!

Knock knock.

Who's there?

Irish.

Irish who?

Irish you a Merry Christmas!

Why is Santa so fat?

Because he has to eat all the children who wake up early on Christmas morning.

Your Honor, I was arrested for doing my Christmas shopping early.

That's no offense. How early were you doing your shopping?

Before the store opened.

How does Good King Wenceslas order his pizza?

Deep pan, crisp and even.

Why did Santa tune his radio to hip hop?

He wanted to improve his wrapping skills.

Last Christmas, I gave you my heart and the very next day

didn't turn out too well because I needed it to live.

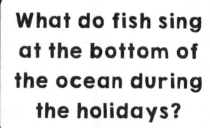

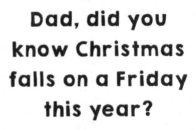

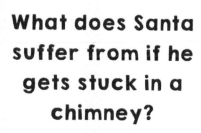

What did the dog say when he spotted the Christmas tree?

Finally, indoor plumbing!

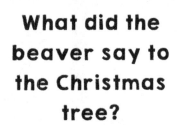

After Mary gave birth to Jesus,

both were in stable condition.

Which of Santa's reindeers has the worst manners?

Rude Olph.

The Three Wise Men *sound* very generous but you've got to remember

those gifts were joint Christmas *and* birthday presents.

When I was a kid we were so poor,

that on Christmas morning we only exchanged glances.

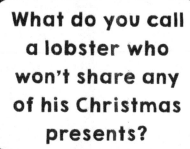

What do you call a lobster who won't share any of his Christmas presents?

Shellfish.

Are we having grandma for Christmas dinner?

No, I think we'll stick with turkey.

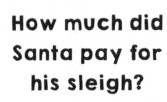

How much did Santa pay for his sleigh?

Nothing, it was on the house!

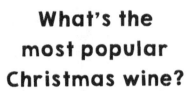

How do you know when the snowwoman is mad at the snowman?

She gives him the cold shoulder.

Santa just saw your social media pictures.

This Christmas you'll be getting clothes and better decision-making skills.

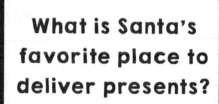

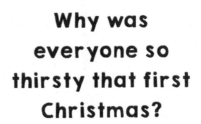

Why was everyone so thirsty that first Christmas?

No well, no well.

Dad, I can't get to the chocolates in my Advent calendar.

Foiled again.

What is the best Christmas present in the world?

A broken drum, you just can't beat it!

What do you get if you eat Christmas decorations?

Tinsilitis!

How many gifts can Santa squeeze into an empty stocking?

One. It's not empty after that.

This will be the third year in a row that my in-laws will come over for Christmas.

I think this time we should let them in.

Why are pirates the best gift givers?

Because they arrrrrrr!

What did the snowman say on his birthday?

This carrot cake tastes like boogers.

I told my dad to go to Amazon to do his Christmas shopping.

He called me two days later, lost in Brazil.

What did the snowman say to the hostile carrot?

Get out of my face!

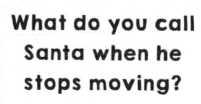

What do you call Santa when he stops moving?

Santa Pause.

What did the Gingerbread Man put on his bed?

A cookie sheet.

I love Christmas snacks: baby cookies, baby crackers and

baby cheeses.

Why are Christmas trees so bad at sewing?

They always drop their needles!

I know you wanted a sweater for Christmas,

but I only could afford a card again.

Who delivers presents to baby sharks at Christmas?

Santa Jaws.

We decorated our bathroom with Christmas items.

Now it's full of toilet trees.

'Twas the night before Christmas and all through the house,

everyone was on a device.

 There are four stages of man:

 Believe in Santa Claus.

 Don't believe in Santa Claus.

 Be Santa Claus.

 Look like Santa Claus.

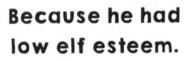

Knock knock.

Who's there?

Hannah.

Hannah who?

♪ Hannah partridge in a pear tree... ♪

Why does Santa Claus go down the chimney on Christmas Eve?

Because it "soots" him!

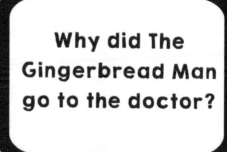

Why did The Gingerbread Man go to the doctor?

He was feeling crummy.

Where do Santa Claus and the elves keep their money?

In a snow bank.

What would you call an elf who has just won the lottery?

Welfy.

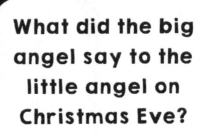

What do you call a kid who doesn't believe in Santa?

A rebel without a Claus.

Knock knock.

Who's there?

Snow.

Snow who?

Snow use, I've already forgotten the joke.

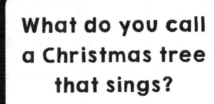

What do you call a Christmas tree that sings?

Spruce Springsteen.

What is an
atheist's favorite
Christmas movie?

"Coincidence on
34th Street".

What did the elf say was the first step in using a Christmas computer?

"First, yule log on."

Made in the USA
Coppell, TX
04 December 2021

67113413R00059